TABLE OF CONTENTS

i

# CONFLICT RESOLUTION IN IRAQ:  A TWO TRACK PROCESS

As is evident with the situation in Iraq, finishing a war is more problematic than starting one.  Conflict termination was achieved in approximately 30 days of combat, but conflict resolution does not appear imminent.  According to U.S. Secretary of Defense Donald Rumsfeld, the U.S.-led coalition is attempting unfamiliar and unique methods to resolve the conflict.[1]  Recent debate, however, has raised tremendous concern whether conflict resolution in Iraq will ever evolve with current U.S. policy.  As a result, U.S. President George Bush and his Administration continue to revise U.S. policy in Iraq.

The debate between the U.S.-led coalition and its installed Iraqi Governing Council (IGC), between the U.S. Administration and Congress, and between the U.S. and the UN exposes disagreements concerning the legitimacy of U.S. policy and the effect that policy has or will have on Iraqi sovereignty.  In this environment, three policy options have emerged on how to attain conflict resolution: the initial U.S. policy, a proposal made by several members of the IGC, and France's proposal.  (There are many nations and entities that argue the same issues as the French, but for simplicity sake, the third policy option will be referred to as the French option.)  Following a brief introduction of each policy option, and an historical examination of three conflict resolution case studies involving the U.S., this paper will propose a solution that can gain legitimacy in every facet of this project, and resolve the conflict in Iraq.

With the hope of developing the appropriate approach to conflict resolution in Iraq, the Bush Administration has recently modified several milestones while simultaneously searching for a valid UN role in the process.  One such milestone is the transfer of political responsibility to the IGC by 1 July 2004.  And, as a re-entry point for the UN, Kofi Annan, the UN Secretary General, recently announced that he would send a mission back to Iraq as soon as its safety could be assured.  These step further indicate a realization that U.S. policy in Iraq must achieve legitimacy with Iraqis, within the Region, and in the International community.  Only after this is achieved, will the U.S.–led coalition assist Iraq reestablish sovereignty, and create a peaceful Iraq capable of positive contributions to the region and the world.

## OVERVIEW:  THE FRAMEWORK FOR REESTABLISHING IRAQI SOVEREIGNTY

The past does not always provide a clear path for the future, but it is all we have from which to draw useful lessons.  Before venturing into the current situation, one has to have some appreciation for modern U.S. intervention into sovereign entities and its previous involvement in Iraq.  Specifically, it is important to appreciate lessons from recent conflict resolution attempts, as well as what occurred in Iraq after Operations Desert Shield and Storm against Saddam Hussein's regime in 1991.

A review reveals that the U.S has interposed or intervened in other countries' internal affairs since the early 1800s when the Marines forcefully boarded and scuttled the *Philadelphia*. This action precipitated the Barbary Wars against the North African pirates and resulted in the establishment of freedom of the seas. Many interventions delivered tangible benefits like this, but generally the overall results of these forays are mixed.[2]

Within the last century, the U.S. has attempted to resolve conflicts by intervening in other countries' affairs sixteen times; twelve of these attempts were pursued unilaterally. [3] Clearly, the U.S. is active in this arena. But this does not mean it has been very successful. On the contrary, the lessons learned from these ventures highlight that conflict resolution is difficult at best.[4] Likewise, the poor results from unilateral U.S. actions signify that tremendous challenges would confront the U.S. in Iraq. Using U.S. history as a guide, gaining legitimacy in Iraq and in the region, especially unilaterally, would be an extremely challenging endeavor, and if not done properly, could fail entirely.

When it last intervened militarily in Iraq, the U.S. garnered overwhelming international support and consent. In 1991, a U.S.-led coalition ejected Iraqi troops from Kuwait. Saddam Hussein's forces were routed. He and his generals had no alternative but to sign a cease-fire agreement, and meet the severe demands of the international community. The coalition achieved conflict termination in a brief 100-hour war, but did not achieve any resolution to the conflict even after 10 years of a enforcing the agreements by a greatly reduced coalition. Disputes over Iraq's compliance with UN demands for scrapping weapons of mass destruction (WMD) programs and concerns over the execution of the UN oil-for-food programs were two leading causes for international cohesion disappearing.[5] Due to diminished international cohesion, Saddam Hussein was able to violate practically every condition spelled out in the cease-fire agreement and in the concomitant United Security Council Resolutions UNSCR).[6]

The tragedies of "9/11" left Americans with a new sense that the world was a dangerous place. The old casualness toward broken promises was no longer acceptable. Beginning in early 2002, even more so than the previous Administration, President Bush began exerting pressure on Iraq to fulfill its agreement, or pay the consequences. After a year of political efforts and military posturing, without any change in the status quo, the Bush administration insisted on real disarmament or a change in regime. When the former did not occur, the latter did. But, the international solidarity that existed in 1991 was now absent. The ensuing military action was

2

undertaken despite the lack of international support and the meager historical record of unilateral U.S. experiences in conflict resolution.

Prior to the U.S. led coalition commencing its military operation in March of 2003, President Bush directed the U.S. Department of Defense (DoD) to form a post-war planning group for Iraq. This group, the Office of Reconstruction and Humanitarian Assistance (ORHA), positioned itself in the region, and moved into Iraq behind the military offensive, and attempted to lay the foundation for the coalition's conflict resolution operations.[7] Within three months, the President and Secretary of Defense determined that the post-conflict Iraqi environment was much more complex than anticipated, and determined that ORHA was not the appropriate organization to accomplish the mission assigned to it. For this, and various additional reasons that are beyond the scope of this paper, the President dissolved ORHA.[8] In its place, the U.S. established a Coalition Provisional Authority (CPA), a more functionally oriented organization that could potentially address the complexities of Iraq from the perspective of an occupying power more appropriately.[9]

Within days of announcing the end of combat operations or conflict termination, the President appointed the Honorable L. Paul Bremer as his personal envoy to Iraq to oversee, direct, and coordinate all U.S. programs and activities in Iraq, except those under the command of CENTCOM. Together, under the direction of the U.S. Secretary of Defense, Mr. Bremer and the Commanding General for CENTCOM would help the President "protect the American people and support freedom throughout the world."[10] Four days later, the Secretary of Defense designated the President's envoy to Iraq as the Administrator of the CPA with responsibility for the temporary governance of Iraq.[11] With these memoranda, the President and his Administration established the framework upon which the U.S. and, it was hoped, the international community would reestablish Iraqi sovereignty, and resolve the conflict in Iraq.

## TRANSITION TO CONFLICT RESOLUTION: IS THERE LEGITIMACY?

Before analyzing conflict resolution in Iraq, one has to understand the difference between conflict termination and conflict resolution. Conflict termination, as defined by Peter Wallensteen alludes to victory of one party over another. One party dominates the other and is able to impose its order on the other.[12] U.S. Joint Doctrine states that conflict termination is achieved by applying military force towards an objective that defines the peace. Simply stated, conflict termination is nothing more than the cessation of hostilities, which establishes the condition for conflict resolution.[13] What is not stated, however, is the dependence of conflict resolution on the condition or nature of the environment at conflict termination.

3

Conflict resolution as defined by Wallensteen is a purposeful search for ways of accommodating explicit interests of the parties in conflict.[14] Conflict resolution is the process of facilitating a solution where the actors no longer feel the need to indulge in conflict activity and feel that the distribution of benefits in the social system is acceptable. [15] In other words, all parties can agree to a path to peace, and are mutually satisfied with the outcome and solution to the disagreement.[16] Using these definitions, one can discern that the official transition between conflict termination and conflict resolution in Operation Iraqi Freedom occurred when President Bush declared that the major fighting was over on 1 May 2003.

Even before 1 May, however, military forces continued to secure the peace throughout Iraq, and align their efforts to harmonize the interagency process and coalesce their endeavors with the civilian participants. As this administrative transition occurred, a series of localized clashes and battles erupted in central Iraq. The difficulty with these seemingly minor battles is that their combined effects were challenging the very legitimacy the U.S. was attempting to gain. The lack of security was distancing or alienating many Iraqi people from the U.S. and its allies, strengthening the non-interventionist position of the non-participating countries, and testing U.S. public support. The U.S.-led coalition struggled simultaneously with securing its presence in the region, finding and defeating an enemy that was hard to define and locate, and trying to win the support, or at least tolerance, of the Iraqi people and the international community. [17]

Inside Iraq the struggle continued as international diplomatic efforts strived to build upon the coalition's successes. A few countries that had vehemently opposed the war came forward to assist. Subsequently, but only due to a series of terrorist bombings directed at several Embassies and the UN headquarters in Baghdad, the assassinations of a Spanish diplomat and a member of the IGC, and attacks against the people of Iraq, did the international community signal consent for post conflict operations in Iraq.[18] The UN Security Council unanimously endorsed UN Security Council Resolution (UNSCR) 1511 which authorized the reconstruction and democratic transition of Iraq. This measure enabled the U.S. to carry out what is largely its vision of Iraq's political future while creating a UN –authorized multinational force under American command. This resolution provided that authority would be turned over to Iraqis only as quickly as Washington deemed them ready. [19] Furthermore, it delivered the potential international legitimacy that the U.S. needed to achieve conflict resolution by endorsing its actions, welcoming the establishment of the IGC, and reinforcing the temporary nature of the CPA. Finally, it demonstrated international agreement on U.S. objectives to help create an internationally recognized, representative government that will exercise the sovereignty of Iraq.[20]

4

Despite apparently securing international legitimacy with this resolution, the international community has not noticeably increased its cooperation, primarily due to the continuing disagreement with the President's persistent demands for exclusive control of the conflict resolution process.  Furthermore, even as security shortcomings have encouraged the UN and international agencies to depart Iraq, military commanders are continuing to struggle against an elusive and complex adversary.  As a result, a divergent civil-military focus has appeared.  The civilian component is involved in winning the peace while the coalition military attempts to win a war that the U.S. cannot afford to lose.[21]  This dichotomy has not produced peace, and the struggle to achieve conflict resolution continues as the blame for the disorderly environment is placed on U.S. policy itself.

As the Administration and its key leaders inside of Iraq modify U.S. policy to achieve success, the dissenting voices grow louder.  The U.S. Presidential election is under way, and the contentious conflict resolution policy is becoming more politicized.  It is essential that the Administration consider various strategic alternatives against the backdrop of the historical lessons learned regarding conflict resolution.  Then the Administration can develop a policy that establishes Iraqi sovereignty in a way that gains legitimacy.

**CONFLICT RESOLUTION IN IRAQ:  THREE ALTERNATIVES**

Security is a key consideration in the three alternatives to conflict resolution that have been promulgated in recent months.  The first alternative, U.S. policy from April to November 2003, created a two-track process, security and politics, under the supervision of the U.S. Department of Defense (DoD).  The policy was centered on the certainty that Iraqis would neither establish nor operate federal institutions until there was security. [22] Functioning political and civic institutions are necessary for establishing legitimacy and re-establishing sovereignty.  Without these institutions, the U.S. believed that long-term stability would not flourish, and Iraqi lives would not improve in material terms.  The absence of stability and improvement would discourage any Iraqi support of the ongoing reconstruction effort.[23]  Only when coalition, and Iraqi security forces created a safe environment would the Iraqis participate in conflict resolution.  Originally, the security effort included a very broad approach - coalition soldiers raiding houses where insurgents and terrorists hide, civilian engineers repairing electrical generators, Iraqi school teachers preparing lessons from textbooks cleansed of Saddam Hussein's indoctrination, and newly trained Iraqi border guards checking passports against lists of terrorists.[24]  Concurrently, with CPA and international assistance, the IGC was producing its own military and security forces.[25]  These forces included the New Iraqi Army, the Iraqi Civil

Defense Corps (ICDC), The Iraqi Police Service (IPS), Border Police and Immigration and Customs Service, and the Facilities Protection Service. After these indigenous security forces were organized, trained, and equipped, the U.S. incorporated elements of them into service. The objective was to incrementally transfer responsibility to the Iraqis. This move created legitimacy with the citizens, and gave Iraqis confidence to pursue civil matters.

As part of this legitimacy in civic matters, the U.S. has already appointed members from Iraq's various factions to the IGC. Together with the U.S., the IGC began to resolve complex questions on the boundaries of the provinces in a federal Iraq, ensuring religious liberty and equality, as well as create the right system of government to manage Iraq's distinctive ethno-religious mix.[26] Additionally, the IGC would oversee the drafting, writing and ratification of the constitution, and coordinate a free and democratic election. Only when all this is accomplished, did the U.S. intend to give Iraq full control of self-governance. The U.S. preferred an orderly process that was neither hurried nor delayed. The initial U.S. estimate was that Iraq would have self-rule within one to two years.

The U.S. recently modified its policy by establishing a political transition suspense of 1 July 2004 and has invited the UN to ascertain if elections can occur sooner. Internal Iraqi factional impatience and challenges to U.S. policy, as well as internal U.S. pressure, compelled the U.S. to take these steps. Meanwhile, international participation and support has grown to nearly 20 nations. Nevertheless, the U.S. maintains that international cooperation and improved burden sharing warrants America's leadership in both tracks, solidifying strategic unity of command of the entire conflict resolution process.[27]

The second alternative is proposed by the IGC and outlines a similar timeline for the transfer of power. The IGC feels that fixing a date to this significant event is essential to establishing legitimacy with its citizens. Therefore, it calls for the transfer to occur in the political track immediately, and in the security track within the year.

The IGC concurs fully with the U.S.'s two-track application and the many procedures; however, the Iraqi organization disagrees with U.S. policy on three counts. First, Iraqis believe a paradox is created by the U.S.-led military coalition in charge of the security track. From this perspective, using the same force that removed Saddam Hussein's regime has resulted in unforeseen challenges to creating a secure environment.[28] Secondly, the IGC feels that Iraqi citizens may perceive a gap in Iraqi sovereignty with a tardy transfer of power.[29] And finally, the Council senses that without rapidly assuming control of the political track, citizens of Iraq and neighboring countries will consider any Iraqi administration as a U.S. puppet.

The IGC alternative calls for a change in the security force composition because the current formations are not conducive to popular support. Various actors ranging from some in the international community and disgruntled Iraqi citizens to remnants of Saddam Hussein's regime and some unknown transnational actors present serious challenges to the coalition's efforts solely because they perceive the U.S. military as an occupying force.[30] Several individuals or groups are spoiling the possibility of law and order and disrupting the peace by taking advantage of the ongoing wholesale transition of the U.S. military contingent. To address this, the IGC proposes the establishment of a multi-ethnic security force deployed around the country and under the unified command of the Iraqi interior ministry. The theory is that if Iraqis see other Iraqis or Arabs directing and operating the security apparatus, the process gains legitimacy.

As for creating legitimacy within the political track, the IGC fears that any perceived gap in Iraqi sovereignty will derail the entire process. Therefore, the IGC wants to send a message to the Iraqi citizens and the world that Iraq has control of its own destiny and together will rapidly move to secure Iraqi sovereignty. The immediate partial turnover of certain elements of the political process, with a phased transition of power attached to a timeline will speed up the entire process, and ultimately ensure lasting conflict resolution.[31] In November 2003, U.S. policy accommodated this timeline, establishing a 1 July 2004 transfer of responsibility in the political track, with the understanding that elections would soon follow. UN analysis, as well as U.S. rhetoric in February 2004, however, raises doubts about the feasibility of this milestone and the possibility for it to be achieved, but the date still stands.[32]

Whereas security matters dominate the initial U.S. policy, the IGC sees that having a more balanced relationship between the security and political tracks is essential. On the other hand, while acknowledging the role of security, the French option sees politics as the critical track for Iraqi sovereignty. To this end, the French assign a larger role to the UN in both the political and security tracks. Without the UN, France does not envision regional nation states and the International Community granting legitimacy to either track. French officials argue that without this regional and international support, the chance for peace in Iraq is greatly reduced.

Like the IGC, France perceives a similar paradox with the U.S.-led coalition at the helm of all security matters. The French President, Jacques Chirac, contends that immediately turning over the political track to the Iraqis will provide a speedy resolution of all security issues. He believes that gaining legitimacy in the political process will reduce the security challenges dramatically and instantly. The answer, therefore, is an international military presence that responds to UN direction, but is under the command of the "main troop contributor."[33] To add legitimacy and encourage Iraqi support, this multi-national approach must assume a peace building posture to send the signal that "we are here to help," and remove the perception of an occupying power.

The French also assign a more crucial role to the UN in the political track. Even though the IGC is considered to lack any mandate from the people due to its structure and selection process, the French proposal provides for imminent transfer of power to the IGC. At the same time, France calls for the UN and the IGC to create a "provisional" Iraqi government that will assume the political responsibilities within 90 days. Without true representation of the people, the French believe that Iraqis will not be confident that the government is addressing its citizens' needs, or that the lives of Iraqis will improve materially. [34]

The French alternative postulates that UN leadership is a necessary precondition to the solution of Iraq's ills, and that Iraqi demonstration of actual political control is, even if under UN auspices, the indispensable hallmark of sovereignty. President Chirac envisions an expanded UN presence in Iraq, with greater participation in the country's political transition, and a rapid transition to an Iraqi authority with real power. He believes this is the key to returning sovereignty to Iraq and creating legitimacy with Middle East neighbors and with the rest of the international community. [35]

In all three alternatives, the cornerstone is the legitimating effort in Iraq. To this end, policies focus on the two principal tracks to conflict resolution – politics and security. The distinction among the three options is threefold - the relationship between the two tracks, the timeline for the transition of power in both tracks, and the effect that the relationship and timeline have on building legitimacy of purpose. Whereas the security track is essential to U.S. policy, each track is equal in the IGC option, and the political track takes primacy in the French approach. As for self-governance, U.S. policy calls for a gradual process, the IGC calls for a more rapid transition, and the French demand an immediate transition of power. And finally, the proponent of each of these options believes that its alternative will achieve legitimacy more effectively and efficiently, and that only its proposed process will lead to a lasting peace.

**U.S. HISTORY LESSON: PREVIOUS ATTEMPTS AT CONFLICT RESOLUTION**

Recent history provides several useful examples to derive lessons learned, anticipate challenges, and gain insights involved with conflict resolution. Three such operations are: operations in Germany after World War II, in Bosnia after the end of the Cold War, and in Kosovo soon thereafter. Each provides valuable lessons regarding challenges to the political and security tracks, options as to who should be in charge of each track, methods to involve indigenous people of Iraq, and steps that can be taken to secure the environment.

**Germany**: Operations in Germany known as ECLIPSE are pertinent less for similarities than because U.S. policy-makers seem to have derived most of their theories from ECLIPSE.[36] The two Balkans cases have a great many similarities with the Iraq environment. In Iraq, as there were in Bosnia and Kosovo, there are negative outside influences throughout the immediate region, there is no consensus on the nature of the target nation, there is a deeply fractured polity with entrenched sectarian and ethnic disorder, there are some locals that have experience with the local administration, and most important, the project represents an overly ambitious endeavor.[37]

Despite the many differences between Iraq in 2003 and Germany in 1945, there are still useful lessons that the U.S. Administration can apply. One of the foremost lessons is including the local population in the political process even after the removal of the corrupt regime in charge of the country. A second important lesson is that security operations provide the umbrella under which political efforts are pursued.

In ECLIPSE, Germany was rebuilt from the bottom up, starting with local elections and councils. After responsibility and authority was transferred to the indigenous leaders at the local level, the Allies focused on state governments. Only after the lower administrations were in place were national elections considered. This bottom-up effort fostered legitimacy within each community first, facilitating local support for the Allied efforts.[38]

Reestablishing the judicial system was very challenging due to the thorough corruption brought on by the Nazi party. The initial plans called for complete removal of the Nazi party, or De-Nazification, regardless the level of support any individual provided to the regime. The U.S. changed this method, and found ways to retain and return to their positions, qualified senior managers who did not have a proven record of corruption. The Allies developed a vetting mechanism to screen and include former Nazi party members after the German national provided an oath of allegiance. This enabled experienced administrators to participate in the development of the local civil institutions including the entire legal spectrum.[39]

After selecting several educated and loyal Germans, the Allies trained them to be lay judges and lawyers. This proved most beneficial, enabling the rapid return of law and order. Furthermore, to perform routine governmental functions, the U.S. and the Allies relied primarily on indigenous bureaucracies.[40] By using respectable, local individuals that were loyal to the cause, the Allies got the government "moving" quickly, concurrently legitimizing the process. To enhance the budding legitimacy, the U.S. approached the economic solutions holistically. The efficient and large humanitarian effort combined with the economic policies and the establishment of government services improved the quality of living immediately and for the long-term benefit of the Germans. All were managed by German nationals and visible to the Germans and their neighbors. Since the citizens could see material improvement for them and their nation, they openly participated and supported the endeavor.[41]

ECLIPSE planners understood that effective state institutions evolve out of the nation's social structure, cultural norms, and distribution of political power. Therefore, they did not radically alter the existing constitution, governmental agencies and subordinate programs. Furthermore, they empowered the trusted German nationals to adjust programs and policies to reflect their identity and culture. These uniquely German institutions coupled with the open support for the political aspects, the large number of U.S. and Allied military forces and the establishment of a strong constabulary force effectively preempted most resistance.[42] The successful security programs, generous humanitarian effort, along with the highly educated and economically developed society effectively established Germany's acceptance back into the international community and helped to stabilize the region.

**Bosnia-Herzegovina:** The advent of the Cold War closely followed the end of World War II. Although the Cold War was a source of international tensions, it also tended to keep many potential conflicts 'on ice.' Once the cold war ended, new hostilities emerged, often between different ethnic, racial or religious groups. Such hostilities erupted in civil wars and international conflicts including the former Yugoslavia and Bosnia-Herzegovina. This environment in Bosnia resulted in different useful lessons.

The civil war in Bosnia ceased with the signing of the General Framework Agreement for Peace (GFAP). The nations in the Contact Group – U.S., Russia, Britain, France, and Germany – and their Peace Implementation Council (PIC) agreed to a NATO-led military force completing the military aspects of the GFAP, and the Office of the High Representative (OHR) supervising the civilian effort.[43] The military effectively achieved their GFAP objectives within the year, enforcing the peace and providing a generally secure area for the civilian aspects to take hold. The OHR-led efforts were less effective.[44] The PIC provided final authority in theater to OHR regarding interpretation of the Agreement on the Civilian implementation of the Peace Settlement. The OHR's authority, however, did not translate into actual power.[45] As a result, there was a lack of cooperation between the many organizations striving to resolve the civil aspects of the GFAP. This further weakened the lack of unity of effort between NATO and the OHR ; the two tracks – military and civil.[46] In order to advance the peace, the military expanded its mission into the civilian aspects of nation building.

10

Two factors that further exacerbated the challenging situation were the premature elections and the further expansion of organized crime. Both came as a result of the joint civil – military failure to establish viable democratic institutions early. Due to the U.S. Administration pushing for a one-year military operation, the OHR imposed an abbreviated timeline for elections. Therefore, elections were held at every level of society prior to the establishment of government institutions. Afterward, there was an enormous amount of time and energy devoted to removing several democratically elected officials suspected of war crimes. This resulting void in governance and associated absence of government services opened the door even wider for expansive smuggling and illegal trafficking. Therefore, the local citizenry saw no benefit to the efforts of the international community and many took matters into their own hands, exacerbating the economic problems and shortcoming of the civil programs.[47]

Some additional deficiencies of the OHR involvement were its inability to curb the discordant and irredentist objectives of the external Serbian and Croatian governments, and to strengthen the constitutional authority of the Bosnian national government.[48] Bosnia's neighbors and the indecisiveness of Bosnia's elected officials were undermining the civil aspects of the GFAP, reducing any possibility of achieving legitimacy with the Bosnians, regardless to which faction they belonged, and throughout the region.[49]

The military coalition, on the other hand, met its objectives. One facilitating aspect was its placement of representative military forces. Russians and Turks forces, for example, were situated in areas where they immediately accrued legitimacy in the eyes of the locals. The international military cooperation signaled international resolve as well as indicated to the Bosnians that the military was not an occupying force. Nevertheless, near immediate military successes were not enough to overcome the lack of unity of effort between the civil and military tracks and the inadequacy of some UN programs, and the military gradually expanded its role. This "mission creep" was necessitated by OHR deficiencies: apprehending war criminals and removing suspect members of the regime was not accomplished quickly enough, and in some cases, not at all; not reducing or destroying vitriolic nationalist radio stations fueled interethnic hatred; finally the UN's agency for enforcing law and order, the International Police Task Force (IPTF), took eight months to form, and then took another four years to influence the local police forces.[50] It took far too long to stabilize security throughout the country, which was not conducive to reintegrating the country, ultimately aborting any legitimacy.

The military continues to serve successfully in Bosnia, and the civilian efforts have improved immeasurably, sustaining international financial assistance that continues to play a key, positive role in economic policymaking. But, the initially unsuccessfully coordinated or

11

directed civilian efforts, and the rather slothful development of their associated program did not reduce the political divisiveness that fueled the conflict in the first place, and weakened the local security environments, specifically with regards to containing illegal economic activities. Additionally, the civilian efforts failed to change the attitudes of indigenous peoples in terms of legitimizing the goals and objectives of the international community. Furthermore, leaders in neighboring countries did not support, and openly contradicted the international efforts. Together, these hurdles have delayed conflict resolution in Bosnia, and thus the establishment of Bosnian sovereignty. Basically, the GFAP was flawed. As a result, Bosnia with all of its factions and fractures has still not fully reentered the international community after nine years of international efforts.

**Kosovo:** It is worth noting that Kosovo's autonomy had been under threat since prior to the civil war in Bosnia-Herzegovina when Mr. Milosevic, the Serbian President, effectively established police rule. Mr. Milosevic removed ethnic Albanians from most positions of responsibility, thus effectively ending self-rule. The Albanian response was to create parallel Albanian-only structures and to disassociate from the Yugoslav's systems, creating the obvious impulse for complete independence. The evidence of subsequent systematic brutality against unarmed Albanian civilians in Kosovo (including women and children) is compelling. Absent the complete withdrawal of the Serb security forces, intervention was necessary to protect them from further atrocities. The Serb minority in Albania though had not been immune from reprisal attacks and their safety was also a paramount consideration. Concern for widespread starvation and death from the onset of a Balkan winter finally compelled NATO to intervene militarily. [51]

Many nations outside of NATO disagreed with this intervention. Even within NATO, there was serious disagreement on the prosecution of the intervention. After several weeks of an air war, political pressure on Mr. Milosevic led to conflict termination in Kosovo. At this phase, many nations beyond the circle of NATO offered to help with conflict resolution in Kosovo.

Many of the challenges that existed during the conflict subsided in this subsequent stage. The degree of collaboration and burden sharing among the international participants indicated international legitimacy despite the disagreement within the same community over military operations. Many of the same nations participating in Bosnia did so in Kosovo too; leadership in the two tracks, however did not. Like Bosnia, NATO led the security aspects. Applying lessons learned from the failure of OHR in Bosnia, however, the UN became the leading agent in the political efforts. Planners properly applied some additional lessons from Bosnia, which has been significant to the successful operations

Unlike Bosnia, there is less of a gap between the two tracks; unity of effort is clearly more evident. The civil and military aspects of conflict resolution in Kosovo may be under different management, but both work tirelessly to ensure the mandates and capabilities of the two functional entities overlap sufficiently to reduce the possibility of, or minimize any existing gap. As an example, the military, or KFOR, assumed responsibility for all security operations immediately after arriving, and continued these programs until the UN civil police forces, or UNMIK were ready. Despite the extensive time it took for the UN to stand up UNMIK and assume responsibility, contributing militaries in KFOR applied significant efforts training local authorities to perform law enforcement and general maintenance of public security. [52]

KFOR also assumed responsibility for humanitarian efforts upon its entrance into Kosovo. Planners had the forethought to ensure a transition to UN coordination and control occurred as soon as the UN and the international agencies became operational. This assisted in developing a perception within the local communities that KFOR forces were truly present to resolve the peace, and not for some ulterior motive. KFOR conducting both security and humanitarian services could have created the paradox identified by the IGC and the French concerning U.S. efforts in Iraq. But, the opposite was true.[53] There was some confusion within the civilian community as to whom they should turn for assistance even after the UN agencies were in place; but, ultimately, the indigenous people provided support legitimizing the combined efforts of KFOR and the international agencies under UN control.[54]

Too many challenges in the establishment of local governments, however, have stunted progress with regard to the transfer of control to Kosovars. This process has been complicated due to the desire of the locals to follow those who led them in the resistance movement, and KFOR and the UN ignoring this issue. Slowly, and with much difficulty, the UN appointed successors and assumed the unpopular responsibility of displacing "so-called" democratically appointed officials. In addition, other challenges arose from the absence of any independent government prior to the conflict. It took much intervention on the part of the UN to establish the necessary agencies. Initially, expatriates staffed these government services. Subsequently, however, appointed locals were paired with these outsiders for training and familiarization as well as ensuring these agencies reflected the nation's unique characteristics.

In short, the perception of the Kosovars has changed, but due to the planned delay in determining Kosovo's final status, to the steady transfer of civil and military responsibilities to local control, and to strong international efforts to strengthen the support throughout the region.

13

Their view of the immense international effort and interest, as well as the fact that they are now in charge, has persuaded them to trust the UN and NATO more, and join in resolving the issues, legitimizing the collective international civil and military efforts. This distinct method that drew on the lessons learned from Bosnia-Herzegovina conflict resolution led to elections within two years, and an economic recovery not seen since the post-World War II era.[55] Very quickly, the multi-national effort established legitimacy within the local communities, throughout Kosovo and the Balkans region as well as in the international community; and the province is being re-integrated into the region.

## ANALYSIS: ENSURING CONFLICT RESOLUTION IS NO MIRAGE

The three historical case studies are useful in analyzing the three alternatives considered for resolving the conflict in Iraq. From the perspective of all three case studies, the current U.S. policy of assigning DoD as the single office for coordinating security and political activities provides a valuable unity of command that solidifies the effort and eliminates any strategic gap between the political and security tracks much as occurred in ECLIPSE. This paper is not making a proposition that DoD is or is not the appropriate office to be managing conflict resolution in Iraq, but properly applying this principle, unity of command, at the strategic level will ensure that actions in either area will be synchronized and complementary. Another useful element is the CPA working closely with the IGC to ensure all political and civic institutions are functional, and that institutional checks and balances are emplaced before transferring power. This should ensure Iraq evolves into a viable nation state. However, keeping the U.S. selected IGC as the sole form of Iraqi federal government while the U.S. retains sole command of the overall operation might create the perception that Iraq is a U.S. puppet and that the U.S. has ulterior motives. This is unlike the experiences in Bosnia and Kosovo in which the UN was employed effectively and eliminated any perception of a single dominant or controlling nation in charge of all political and military activities. Nothing could be worse for Iraq's future than the creation of a puppet government unable to keep the peace and susceptible to the charge that it was sovereign in name only. [56]

Removing all Iraqi military and civilian leaders with ties to the Baathist regime in the manner of the German occupation without question raises additional challenges to U.S. motives in the region. This ultimately jeopardizes both security and political efforts, and creates an immediate pool of recruits for those who oppose U.S. action. Furthermore, keeping the U.S. DoD as the singular leader of all conflict resolution procedures can strengthen the perception that the U.S. military is an occupying force with the goal of creating a U.S. protectorate.

14

Modifying policy by applying the strengths from the IGC COA can eliminate this perception, particularly important in an environment which, unlike World War II, did not involve total capitulation at the end of a prolonged struggle.

One such strength in the IGC COA is the rapid but incremental transfer of federal political power to the Iraqis. As we derived from the ECLIPSE and Kosovo lessons, strengthening the local governments early conveys legitimacy to the indigenous people much more quickly. The resulting support the locals may give to outsiders is beneficial to both the security as well as the political efforts. As was evident in all three case studies, however, care must be given to ensure that the system reflects Iraqi customs, traditions, and psyche. Ultimately, this will enhance nation-wide participation in building lasting political and civic institutions. Therefore, giving the IGC control over this process sooner rather than later is worth considering. If this is done, the U.S. or UN can remain involved after the earlier transfer of power and mentor the leaders through the elections. This way, the U.S. can help establish the political institutions, facilitating the development of an appropriate democratic system for the Iraqis, and one that may be acceptable to the U.S., and more importantly, tolerable to Iraq's neighbors.

A second strength of the IGC alternative is that of involving the Iraqi interior minister in security matters. As attempted in the two Balkans cases, a rapid movement toward indigenous security forces providing protection to the well being of their own, will strengthen the coalition's efforts and eliminate the perception of an occupying force with ulterior motives. Furthermore, an engaged minister will strengthen the resolve of the Iraqi military and police forces, enhance a speedier transfer of responsibility to Iraq's security forces, and provide practical experience for the assumption of full responsibility a la Kosovo. One weakness of the IGC COA that any policy must avoid is the singular focus on internal legitimacy. As all three historical examples demonstrate, Iraq will not be a relevant entity without the support of the international community, and especially the acceptance of nations within the region. Without such support, the potential exists for neighboring influences to negate progress and create greater impediments to conflict resolution like in Bosnia.

Seeking international consent is the strong suit of the French option. Permitting the UN to have oversight or responsibility for elements of the security and political track will encourage cooperation and participation. UNSCR 1511 indicates international willingness to support, but has not produced much support. The UN accepting the burden of responsibility may just be the impetus needed to garner international burden sharing and involvement in conflict resolution in Iraq. If this potential expansion occurs, having a security force with a larger multi-national presence will increase Iraqi legitimacy, and enhance a positive perception of the military forces. This can certainly be a confidence building measure and quite possibly encourage international acceptance of Iraqi sovereignty.

Expanding international participation, and more importantly oversight of the civil aspects, may enhance the international support, collaboration and burden sharing that is a current weakness of U.S. policy.[57] One glaring weakness in the French alternative, is the risk taken with security operations. The contention that an immediate transition of the political process will inherently create security is too idealistic and belied by the Bosnia and Kosovo experiences. The military force in Iraq has to be capable of suppressing an insurgency, thwarting intra-and inter-factional violence, as well as proactively interrupting terrorist threats. A weak security force is dangerous to the fragile entity that exists today. Solving the security problems by rebuilding the Iraqi Police, Army, Civil Defense Corps, Border Police and Immigration and Customs Service, as well as the Facilities Protection Service must be the Coalition's highest priority.[58] Only when the Iraqis believe that Saddam Hussein's regime has truly collapsed and, like in Germany, that national and international criminals are being captured and prosecuted will Iraqis participate in the process free of persecution. Potentially, Iraqi citizens will finally perceive that they can govern themselves and take an active role in developing their own political institutions.

Any policy chosen must involve the indigenous people of Iraq, and effectively secure the environment to instill legitimacy, or conflict resolution will be a mirage, superficial and short-lived. Iraqi society has to have more than "hope" to openly embrace the international efforts as legitimate.

## RECOMMENDATION: IRAQ, AN INSPIRATION TO THE MIDDLE EAST

Given the current alternatives and the evidence of the three case studies, it is apparent that the U.S.-led coalition retaining primacy of the security track until there is a stable environment and Iraq security forces are operational is paramount for success. The lack of security could destroy any effort in the political track, and needs to be brought under control immediately. But, as in Bosnia and Kosovo, and the French alternatives, this issue should be resolved initially with an international police and military force that simultaneously provides security, and teaches and trains the entire Iraqi security apparatus including the national military. These intervening multi-national forces should initially operate under U.S. command and control. Then, in keeping with the IGC approach, these intervening forces should work jointly with and then for the Iraqi interior ministry. Finally, there must be a plan to hand off responsibility locally and incrementally starting from the multi-national police and military forces to the indigenous security forces, and then from the U.S. command to the Iraqi interior minister.

Regardless of where the responsibility lies at any given point, these security forces cannot exclude former regime members, especially at the local level, as long as they are loyal to the security effort. Similarly, the political process cannot prohibit qualified senior managers who do not have a proven record of corruption and abuse, even if they were members of the Baath party, and especially if they were not senior members. As Nazi officials proved to be in post-war Germany, the Baathists may better understand the previous security and political apparatus benefiting the overall effort, and again like the Nazis, may potentially provide valuable information on the current threats to stability. This element must jointly hunt for, apprehend, detain, and prosecute criminals from the previous regime, or those who violently oppose the ongoing national effort. This arrangement with this focus will build legitimacy with the Iraqis at the local level, and may encourage several more nations to provide assistance, especially those with a mutual interest in Iraq's stability, thereby furthering the legitimacy in the country and creating legitimacy within the region.

Any U.S. policy must account for the long-standing issues between the various internal and external factions before introducing any regional military presence into Iraq. As in both Balkans operations, however, proper placement of these regional forces can facilitate a sense of trust or legitimacy with the local population. Additionally, employing security forces from regional contributors may counteract any negative influence precipitated by Iraq's neighbors, as well as diminish the external security problems.[59] It may be risky considering the volatility of the region. But a security structure that includes regional police and military forces should reduce the complex security challenges in Iraq and legitimize conflict resolution operations for the contributing nations. Furthermore, it will embolden local Iraqi legitimacy when Iraqis see numerous international uniforms helping to secure their well being, which ultimately contributes to the political and civil pursuits

As for the political track, this recommendation is aligned closely with the French option. First, the UN needs to be the lead agency. The UN will not necessarily do a better job than the U.S., nor will it be less bureaucratic. And, it will slightly weaken the benefits of the current unity of command. But, giving the UN responsibility for the political aspects will enhance worldwide relationships, and ensure that regional powers do not perceive Iraq as a U.S. puppet or that the U.S. has ulterior motives. Drawing from the Bosnia and Kosovo blueprints, the U.S. DoD or military commander, and subsequently the Iraqi Interior Minister, can make up for the unity of command sacrifices if they work closely with the appointed UN Administrator to ensure unity of effort. Once this arrangement is completed, the UN needs to assist the IGC establish a truly representative interim government. The UN must then consider identifying local members despite their previous allegiance to Saddam Hussein, and train them to execute some responsibility, as well as empower them to modify the process to reflect their society. This will overwhelmingly reinforce the process since it will be familiar to the Iraqi people.

This representative government must have no appearance of any U.S. puppet strings. Together with UN supervision and counsel, this interim government can draft, write, and implement a constitution, conduct elections, and create a democratic government and society. Once Iraqi citizens see material improvement in their own lives as well as a uniquely Iraqi national effort with international support towards improving their government, legitimacy within Iraq will flourish. Furthermore, this same international effort will strengthen the region and give a sense of worldwide ownership to the material improvement in Iraq, quite possibly altering the tensions in the Middle East altogether.

In a recent appearance at the UN, and during the 2004 State of the Union Address, President Bush highlighted the importance of a democratic Iraq that can use its newfound power to inspire the Middle East instead of destabilizing it.[60] He and his Administration have often stated that the U.S.-led coalition invaded Iraq in part to defend the credibility of the UN. Furthermore, the administration has suggested that the UN should assist in developing a constitution, training civil servants, and conducting free and fair elections.[61] This vision will come true only when the Iraqi citizens have confidence that their government can secure itself, that their government has the power to independently resolve their concerns to their liking, that they collectively enjoy equal rights under the law, and can see their own individual material improvement. In other words, this can only be done through legitimizing the process in the eyes of the Iraqi citizens themselves, those within the region, and throughout the international community.

## CONCLUSION: INNOVATIVE AND FLEXIBLE POLICY

Currently, there are factions within Iraq, the international community, and the U.S. Congress that view U.S. policy as inappropriate or insufficient. Regardless of these disparate views, there has to be a purposeful search for ways to accommodate the explicit interest of all parties, inside and outside of Iraq, especially those with a mutual interest in the region, or there will never be conflict resolution. And, without agreement among these factions, the entire resolution process may stagnate.[62] Adopting the proposed composite U.S.-IGC-French policy alternative will enable the establishment of common goals and objectives, a coherent framework for conflict resolution, and complement the mandate for the mission in Iraq. This will hasten the legitimacy of international purpose in Iraq, the return of Iraqi sovereignty, the establishment of a democratic and stable Iraq, and the initiation of peaceful overtures in the Middle East.

Early in the conflict, the international community assumed that the war plan was a failure as the offensive temporarily stalled. But, by executing an innovative and flexible war plan, it took only 21 days for the U.S.-led military coalition to enter Baghdad.[63] Soon afterwards, President Bush announced that the coalition forces clearly won the "war," achieving conflict termination. Since then, the expanding U.S.-led coalition has turned its attention to conflict resolution. After several weeks of battling for "peace," resolution does not appear imminent, and similar cries of failure are reverberating throughout the world. The U.S. will not quiet the dissenting voices by blindly adhering to current U.S. policy, by going it alone, or simply by reaching agreement with the IGC. The current administration has to reflect on previous U.S. conflict resolution attempts, and be bold enough to design and execute an innovative and flexible "peace" plan in the shadows of a similarly designed "war" plan. Only then will it achieve agreement among the U.S., the Iraqis, and the International Community. This composite policy, by involving the UN, a multi-national security force, and incrementally transferring control of both tracks to the Iraqis more quickly than currently planned, will produce long lasting conflict resolution in Iraq, and potentially stabilize the region.


WORD COUNT= 8,273

# ENDNOTES

[1] Donald Rumsfeld, "Beyond 'Nation–Building,'" *Washington Post*, 25 September 2003, 1.

[2] Max Boot, *The Savage Wars of Peace, Small Wars and the Rise of American Power* (New York: Basic Books, 2002), 3-6.

[3] Minxin Pei and Sara Kasper, *Lessons from the Past: The American Record on Nation Building,* (Pittsburgh: Carnegie Endowment for International Peace, May 2003), 1-7.

[4] Ibid.

[5] Alan W. Dowd, "Thirteen Years: the Causes and Consequences of the War in Iraq," *Parameters: US Army War College Quarterly*, VOL. XXXIII, NO. 3, Autumn 2003, 50-56.

[6] Ibid, 46-48.

[7] Secretary of Defense Donald Rumsfeld, "Support for the Organization of Reconstruction and Humanitarian Assistance," memorandum for Secretaries of the Military Departments, Washington, D.C., 2 April 2003.

[8] Secretary of Defense Donald Rumsfeld, "Designation as Administrator of the Coalition Provisional Authority," memorandum for Presidential Envoy to Iraq, Washington DC: 13 May 2003.

[9] Secretary of Defense Donald Rumsfeld, "Authority of the Administrator of the Coalition Provisional Authority," memorandum for Secretaries of the Military Departments, Washington, D.C., 16 June 2003), 1.

[10] President George W. Bush, "Presidential Envoy to Iraq,' memorandum for The Honorable L. Paul Bremer, Presidential Envoy to Iraq, Washington, D.C., 9 May 2003.

[11] Rumsfeld, "Designation as Administrator of the Coalition Provisional Authority."

[12] Peter Wallensteen, "The Resolution and Transformation of International Conflicts: A Structural Perspective," in *New Directions In Conflict Theory, Conflict Resolution and Conflict Transformation*, ed. Raimo Vayrynen. (London: International Social Science Council, 1991), 129-152.

[13] Joint Chiefs of Staff, *Joint Doctrine for Campaign Planning*, Joint Pub 5-00.1. (Washington, D.C.: U.S. Joint Chiefs of Staff, 25 January 2002), II-4-II-5.

[14] Wallensteen, 129-152.

[15] Carl G. Jacobsen with Kai Frithjof Brand-Jacobsen. "Peacemaking as Realpolitik, Conflict Resolution and Oxymoron: the Record, the Challenge " in *Searching for Peace, The Road to Transcend*, eds. Johan Galtung, Carl G. Jacobsen and Kai Frithjof Brand-Jacobsen, (London: Pluto Press, 2000), 27-48.

[16] Wallensteen, 129-152.

[17] "The War Begins," *Global Agenda*, 20 March 2003, 1.

[18] United Nations, Security Council, *Resolution 1511 (2003),* Adopted by the Security Council at its 4844th meeting, 16 October 2003, 2.

[19] Felicity Barringer, "Unanimous Vote By U.N.'s Council Adopts Iraq Plan," *New York Times*, 17 October 2003, 1.

[20] United Nations, 2

[21] Tex DeAtkine, "Preliminary Report On Conditions In Iraq," (Baghdad: December 2004), 2.

[22] Ibid.

[23] Walter Slocombe, "It Takes More Than Guns," *Washington* Post, 14 October 2003, 23.

[24] Ibid.

[25] Noah Feldman, "Democracy, Closer Every Day," *New York Times*, 24 September 2003, 1.

[26] Congress, Senate, Committee on Foreign Relations, *Review of Iraq Policy and Issues: Testimony by Noah Feldman*, 106th Cong., 2d sess., 24 September 2003, 2-4.

[27] Elisabeth Bumiller, "Bush, At UN, Defends Policy Over Iraq," *New York Times*, 24 September 2003, 1.

[28] "Finding A New Path In Iraq," *New York Times*, 24 September 2003, A6.

[29] Betsy Pisik, "Chalabi Minimizes dispute Over Iraqi Self-Rule," *Washington Times*, 25 September 2003, 1.

[30] Dan Murphy, "Despite Some Progress, Iraqis Losing Faith," *Christian Science Monitor,* 14 October 2003, 1.

[31] Barbara Slavin, "Iraqi Council Wants Quick Transfer of Power," *USA Today,* 24 September 2003, 16.

[32] Maggie Farley, U.N. Role In Iraq An open Question For All," *Los Angeles Times*, 31 December 2003, 1.

[33] Feldman, 1.

[34] Colum Lynch, "At The UN, Bush Wins No Fresh Pledges Of Iraq Aid, U.S. Military Action's Value Has Limits, Delegates Say," *Washington Post*, 23 September 2003, 1.

[35] Ibid, 2.

[36] The architects of U.S. policy in Iraq have also made many more connections as they named their operation after that of Germany in 1945; ECLIPSE II.

[37] James Dobbins, et al, *America's Role In Nation-Building: From Germany to Iraq* (Santa Monica, California: RAND, 2003), 149-166.

[38] Dobbins, 3-24.

[39] Hans Binnendijk and Stuart Johnson, *Transforming for Stabilization and Reconstruction Operations,* (Washington DC: National Defense University, December 2003), 34.

[40] Conrad Crane and W. Andrew Terrill, Reconstructing Iraq: Insights, Challenges, and Missions for Military Forces In A Post-Conflict Scenario, (Carlisle, PA: Strategic Studies Institute, 2003), 13-15.

[41] Binnendijk, 34.

[42] Dobbins, 3-24.

[43] Lenard J. Cohen, "Bosnia and Herzegovina: Fragile Peace in a Segmented State," *Current History*, March 1996, 103-107.

[44] Crane, 8-11.

[45] "Is Dayton Failing?: Bosnia 4 Years After Peace Agreement," *ICG Balkans Report*, (Sarajevo: International Crisis Group, 28 October 1999), 42-43.

[46] Dobbins, 87-110.

[47] Crane, 8-11.

[48] Dobbins, 87-110.

[49] Crane, 8-11.

[50] Ibid.

[51] Simon Duke, "The Trouble With Kosovo," *European Institute of Public Administration*, 1998, 5.

[52] Ibid, 111-128.

[53] Crane, 8-11.

[54] Dobbins, 111-128.

[55] Ibid.

[56] Congress, Senate, Committee on Foreign Relations, *Review of Iraq Policy and Issues: Testimony by Noah Feldman*, 106th Cong., 2d sess., 24 September 2003, 2-4.

[57] International Crisis Group, "Iraq: Building a New Security Structure," (Brussels: IGC Middle East Report, 2003), 4-5.

[58] Feldman, 5.

[59] Jim Garamone, "Bosnia Stable, But Peace Still 'Brittle,'" *American Forces Press Service*, 26 September 2003, 3.

[60] Bumiller, 1.

[61] Ibid.

[62] Wallensteen, 151.

[63] Donald Rumsfeld, "Core Principles for a Free Iraq," *Wall Street Journal*, 27 May 2003, A.14.

# BIBLIOGRAPHY

"7 Outa 10 Iraqis Agree U.S. Should Stay Awhile," *New York Daily News*, 14 October 2003, p 1.

Barringer, Felicity. "Unanimous vote By U.N.'s council Adopts Iraq Plan," *New York Times*, 17 October 2003, p 1.

Biden, Joseph R. Jr. and Chuck Hagel. "Winning the Peace." *Washington Post*, 6 April 2003, p B.07.

Binnendijk, Hans and Stuart Johnson. *Transforming for Stabilization and Reconstruction Operations*. National Defense University, Washington D.C., December 2003).

Boose, Donald W., Jr. "The Korean War Truce Talks: A Study n Conflict Termination." *Parameters,* Vol 30, 1, (Spring 2000), 102.

Boot, Max. "The Savage Wars of Peace, Small Wars and the Rise of American Power." New York: Basic Books, 2002.

Borst, Barbara. "Iraq Disputes Dominate General Assembly." *New York Times*, 26 September 2003.

Boule, John R. II. "Operational Planning and Conflict Termination." *Joint Forces Quarterly,* Iss 29, (Autumn 2001-Winter 2002): 97.

Bouras, Stelios and Sebastian Rotella. "War With Iraq; EU Pursues Central Roles for U.N., Itself in Rebuilding of Iraq." *Los Angeles Times*, 18 April 2003, p A.7.

Brand-Jacobsen, Kai Frithjof with Carl G. Jacobsen. "Beyond Mediation: Towards More Holistic Approaches to Peace-building and Peace Actor Empowerment." In *Searching for Peace, The Road to Transcend*, eds. Johan Galtung, Carl G. Jacobsen and Kai Frithjof Brand-Jacobsen, 49-86. London: Pluto Press, 2000.

Bremer, L. Paul III. "The Road Ahead in Iraq – and How to Navigate It," *New York Times*, 13 Jul 2003, p 4, 13.

Brown, Drew. "As Rumors Of New Attacks Roil Baghdad, Few Answers For U.S.," *Philadelphia Inquirer*, 31 October 2003, p 1.

Brun-Rovet, Marianne. "US 'Needs To Enlist Help Of Muslims In War On Terror,'" *London Financial Times*, 31 October 2003, p 10.

Bumiller, Elisabeth. "Bush, At UN, Defends Policy Over Iraq." *New York Times*, 24 September 2003, p 1.

Bush, George W. "Presidential Envoy to Iraq." Memorandum for The Honorable L. Paul Bremer, Presidential Envoy to Iraq. Washington, D.C., 9 May 2003.

Cha, Ariana Eunjung. "Hope And Confusion Mark Iraq's Democracy Lessons," *Washington Post*, 24 November 2003, p 1.

Chalabi, Ahmad. "We've Made Real Progress." *USA Today*, 14 November 2003, p 14.

Chandrasekaran, Rajiv. "Bremer Suppports Iraqi-Led Force," *Washington Post*, 5 November 2003, p 1.

Clover, Charles, Guy Dinmore, and Roula Khalaf. "Bremer Warns On Security Breakdown." *London Financial Times*, 13 November 2003, p 1.

Cohen, Lenard. "Bosnia and Herzegovina: Fragile Peace in a Segmented State," *Current History*, March 1996, 103-112.

Cohen, Richard. "Vietnam It Isn't," *Washington Post*, 30 October 2003, p 23.

Cordesman, Anthony H. "The War after the War in Iraq," *ROA National Security Report*," Washington D.C., October 2003.

Crane, Conrad C, and W. Andrew Terrill. Reconstructing Iraq: Insights, Challenges, and Missions for Military Forces In A Post-Conflict Scenario. Strategic Studies Institute, Carlisle, PA, February 2003.

Cummins, Chip and Neil King Jr. "New Office Created To Rebuild Iraq, Pentagon-Run Operation To Award Contracts in Move to Prioritize Reconstruction," *Wall Street Journal*, 14 October 2003, p 1.

Dao, James and Eric Schmitt." President Picks a Special Envoy to Rebuild Iraq." *New York Times*, 7 may 2003, p A.1.

DeAtkine, Tex. "Preliminary Report On Conditions In Iraq." December 2004.

Dedring, Juergen. "Multilateral Aspects of Conflict Resolution." In *New Directions In Conflict Theory, Conflict Resolution and Conflict Transformation*, ed. Raimo Vayrynen, 153-179. London: International Social Science Council, 1991.

Deutsch, Morton. "Subjective Features of Conflict Resolution: Psychological, Social and Cultural Influences." In *New Directions In Conflict Theory, Conflict Resolution and Conflict Transformation*, ed. Raimo Vayrynen, 26-56. London: International Social Science Council, 1991.

Dobbins, James, John G. McGinn, Keith Crane, Seth G. Jones, Rollie Lal, Andrew Tathmell, Rachel Swanger, and Anga Timilsina. "America's Role In Nation-Building: From Germany to Iraq." Santa Monica, California: RAND, 2003.

"Don't Cut and Run In Iraq," *Chicago Tribune*, 29 October 2003, p 1.

Dowd, Alan W. "Thirteen Years: The Causes and Consequences of the War in Iraq." *Parameters. U.S. Army War College Quarterly,* VOL. XXXIII, No. 3, Autumn 2003, pp46-60.

Dowd, Maureen. "Eyes Wide Shut," *New York* Times, 30 October 2003, p 1.

Duke, Simon. "The Trouble With Kosovo," *European Institute of Public Administration*, 1998, p 5.

Fallows, James. "Blind Into Baghdad," *The Atlantic Monthly*, Jan/Feb 2004. Vol 293, Iss 1: p 52.

Fang, Bay. "Getting Offensive: U.S. Forces Give Up On Hearts and Minds." *U.S. News and World Report.*, 8 December 2003, p 31.

Farley, Maggie. "U.N. Role In Iraq An Open Question For All." *Los Angeles Times*, 31 December 2003, p 1.

Feldman, Noah. "Democracy, Closer Every Day." *New York Times*, 24 September 2003.

"Fickle Interventioists," *Wall Street Journal*, 31 October 2003, p 1.

"Finding A New Path In Iraq." *New York Times*, 24 September 2003.

Flavin, William. "Planning for Conflict Termination and Post-Conflict Success," *Parameters*, VOL. XXXIII, NO3, (Autumn 2003): 95-112

Fram, Alan. "Bush Plan on Iraq Hits Snag in Congress." *Washington Post,* 24 September 2003.

"France: U.S. Exit Would Be Mistake: Fervent voice against attack calls for unity to Rebuild Iraq," *Dallas Morning News*, 31 October 2003, p 1.

Friedman, Thomas L. "Iraqis at The Wheel," *New York Times*, 6 November 2003, p 9.

Friedman, Thomas L. "It's No Vietnam," *New York Times*, 30 October 2003, p 1.

Garamone, Jim. "Bosnia Stable, But Peace Still 'Brittle.'" *American Forces Press Service*, 26 September 2003.

Ghattas, Sam F. "Neighbors Condemn Terrorist Attacks," *Washington Times*, 5 November 2003, p 15.

Goldman John J. and Edwin Chen. "War With Iraq; Annan Talks Up Postwar U.N. Role. *Los Angeles Times*, 8 April 2003, p A.11.

"Governing Iraq." *Middle East Report.* International Crisis Group, Baghdad, 25 August 2003.

Grier, Peter and Faye Bowers. "The Risks of Rapid Iraqification," *Christian Science Monitor*, 6 November 2003, p 1.

Hamburger, Tom, and Greg Jaffe. "White House Debates How Fast To Push Power Transfer In Iraq." *Wall Street Journal*, 12 November 2003, p 13.

Hendawi, Hamza. "Iraqi Constitution Delay Frays Relations." *Associated Press*, 11 November 2003.

Hendren, John. "Pentagon Revising Strategy to Curb Iraqi Resistance," *Los Angeles Times*, 31 October 2003, p 1.

Hoagland, Jim. "Earning From Mistakes In Iraq." *Washington Post*, 19 November 2003, p A.27.

Hoagland, Jim. "Listen to the Iraqis," *Washington Post*, 30 October 2003, p 23.

Ignatieff, Michael, "A Warrior's Honor." New York: Metropolitan Books, 1997.

Ignatius, David. "Bremer's U.N. Lifeline," *Washington Post*, 16 January 2004, p 1.

Ignatius, David. "Minding Iraq's Business," *Washington Post*, 17 October 2003, p 29.

"Important Progress In the War on Terror." *Washington Post*, 9 September 2003, p A.9.

"Iraq Policy in Crisis." *New York Times*, 13 November 2003, p 1.

"Iraq: Building a New Security Structure." *Middle East Report.* International Crisis Group, Baghdad, 21 December 2003.

"Is Dayton Falling? Bosnia 4 years After Peace Agreement." *ICG Balkans Report.* International Crisis Group, Sarajevo, 28 October 1999.

Jacobsen, Carl G. with Kai Frithjof Brand-Jacobsen. "Peacemaking as Realpolitik, Conflict Resolution and Oxymoron: the Record, the Challenge." In *Searching for Peace, The Road to Transcend*, eds. Johan Galtung, Carl G. Jacobsen and Kai Frithjof Brand-Jacobsen, 27-48. London: Pluto Press, 2000.

Jehl, Douglas. "C.I.A. report Suggests Iraqis Are Losing Faith In U.S. Efforts." *New York Times*, 13 November 2003, p 12.

Keegan, John. "Like It Or Not, America Is Becoming An Imperial Power." *London Daily Telegraph*, 13 November 2003, p 1.

Kondracke, Morton M. "Iraq Reconstruction Is A Noble Cause That Mustn't Fail." *Roll Call*, 6 November 2003, p 1.

Labbe, Theola and Coum Lynch. "Red Cross And U.N. To Reduce Iraq Staffs," *Washington Post*, 30 October 2003, p 1.

Lambro, Donald. "Gunning For Strategies," *Washington Times*, 30 October 2003, p 17.

Landay, Jonathan S. "CIA Has A Bleak Analysis Of Iraq." *Philadelphia Inquirer*, 12 November 2003, p 1.

Lugar, Richard G. "A Victory at Risk." *Washington Post*, 22 May 2003, p A.35.

Lynch, Colum. "At The UN, Bush Wins No Fresh Pledges Of Iraq Aid, U.S. Military Action's Value Has Limits, Delegates Say." *Washington Post*, 23 September 2003, p 1.

Lynch, Colum. "New Iraq Proposal offered To U.N.," *Washington Post*, 14 October 2003, p 1.

"Making Policy In Iraq By fits and Starts," *Miami Herald*, 24 November 2003, p 6.

Milbank, Dana. "Bush Is Criticized At UN Over Iraq. Leaders Assail 'Unilateralism.'" *Washington Post*, 24 September 2003, p 25.

Murphy, Dan. "Despite Some Progress, Iraqis Losing Faith." *Christian Science Monitor,* 14 October 2003, p 1.

Nichols, Bill. "U.S. May Ask Security Council to Endores Accelerated Transfer Of Power To Iraqis," *USA Today*, 20 November 2003, p 13.

Pei, Minxin and Sara Kasper. "Lessons from the Past: the American Record on Nation Building," *Carnegie Endowment for International Peace,* May 2003, p 1-7.

Peters, Ralph. "Another Vietnam? No," *New York Post*, 29 October 2003, p 10.

Phinney, Catherine. "Enhancing Conflict Termination Through Problem Solving." *Peacekeeping and International Relations*, 1, (Jan/Feb ´997): p 15.

Pisik, Betsy. "Chalabi Minimizes dispute Over Iraqi Self-Rule." *Washington Times*, 25 September 2003, p 1.

"Postwar, Conflict Continues," *USA Today*, 3 November 2003, p 11.

Rankin, Robert A. "Democrats renew Call for Global Aid, And Control, In Iraq." *Philadelphia Inquirer*, 10 November 2003, p 1.

"Rebuilding Iraq with Iraqis," *New York Times*, 29 June 2003, p 4, 12.

Reid, Robert H. "U.S. Aiming to Stabilize Iraq in 2004." *Washington Times*, 31 December 2004, p 12.

Richburg, Keith B. "France Wants Quicker Shift Of Power In Iraq." *Washington Post*, 14 November 2003, p 25.

Richter, Paul. "U.S. May Delay Iraq Power Transfer." *Los Angeles Times,* 12 February 2004, p 1.

Rubin, Alissa J. "Iraqis See Israel As Culprit In Bombings," *Los Angeles Times*, 30 October 2003, p 1.

Rumsfeld, Donald. "Core Principles for a Free Iraq." *Wall Street Journal*, 27 May 2003, p A.14.

Rumsfeld, Donald. "Designation as Administrator of the Coalition Provisional Authority." Memorandum for Presidential Envoy to Iraq. Washington DC: 13 May 2003.

Rumsfeld, Donald. "Support for the Office of Reconstruction and Humanitarian Assistance." Memorandum for Secretaries of the Military Departments. Washington, D.C., 2 April 2003.

Rumsfeld, Donald. "Beyond 'Nation–Building.'" *Washington Post*, 25 September 2003.

Rumsfeld, Donald. "Authority of the Administrator of the Coalition Provisional Authority." Memorandum for Secretaries of the Military Departments. Washington, D.C., 16 June 2003.

Sachs, Susan. "Threat, Blasts and Pullouts Raise Anxiety IN Baghdad," *New York Times*, 31 October 2003.

Safire, William. "Iraq War III," *New York Times*, 3 November 2003.

Sammon, Bill. "Bush Vows He's 'In Charge,'" *Washington Times*, 14 October 2003, p 1.

Sanger, David E. and Eric Schmitt. "Bush In A Hurry To Train Iraqis In Security Duty," *New York Times, 30 October 2003, p 1.*

Schadlow, Nadia. "War and the Art of Governance," *Parameters*, VOL XXXIII, NO 3 (Autumn 2003): 85-94.

Seabury, Paul and Angela Codevilla. *War, Ends and Means.* New York: Basic Books, Inc, 1989.

Slavin, Barbara. "Iraqi Council Wants Quick Transfer of Power." *USA Today,* 24 September 2003, p 16.

Slevin, Peter, and Vernon Loeb. "Plan to Secure Postwar Iraq Faulted; Pentagon Ignored Lessons From Decade of Peacekeeping, Critics Say." *Washington Post*, 19 May 2003, p A.01.

Slevin, Peter. "U.S. Urged to Modify Approach to Postwar Iraq, Experts Favor Stripping Pentagon of Control." *Washington Post,* 24 September 2003, p 24.

Slocombe, Walter B. "It Takes More Than Guns." *Washington* Post, 14 October 2003, p 23.

The Economist Newspaper Ltd. "*The War Begins.* London: Global Agenda, 20 March 2003, p 1.

Trofimov, Yaroslav, Yochi J. Dreazen, and Carla Anne Robbins. "Latest Iraq Attack Pushes Conflict To Turning Point." *Wall Street Journal*, 13 November 2003, p 1.

"The U.N. Fig Leaf," *Wall Street Journal,"* 17 October 2003, p 1.

"The U.N. Vote On Iraq," *New York Times*, 17 October 2003, p 1.

U.S. Congress, Senate. Committee on Foreign Relations. *Review of Iraq Policy and Issues: Testimony by Noah Feldman*, 106th Cong., 2d sess., 24 September 2003.

U.S. Congress, Senate. Committee on Foreign Relations. *Review of Iraq Policy and Issues: Testimony by Dr. Phebe Marr*, 106th Cong., 2d sess., 24 September 2003.

U.S. Joint Chiefs of Staff. *Doctrine for Joint Operations*. Joint Pub 3-0. Washington D.C.: U.S. Joint Chiefs of Staff, 10 September 2001.

U.S. Joint Chiefs of Staff. *Doctrine for Planning Joint Operations*. Joint Pub 5-0. Washington, D.C.: U.S. Joint Chiefs of Staff, 13 April 1995.

U.S. Joint Chiefs of Staff. *Joint Doctrine for Campaign Planning*. Joint Pub 5-00.1. Washington, D.C.: U.S. Joint Chiefs of Staff, 25 January 2002.

U.S. Joint Chiefs of Staff. *Joint Doctrine for Military Operations Other Than War*. Joint Pub 3-07. Washington D.C.: U.S. Joint Chiefs of Staff, 16 June 1995.

U.S. Joint Chiefs of Staff. *Joint Tactics, Techniques, and Procedures for Peace Operations*. Joint Pub 3-07.3. Washington, D.C.: U.S. Joint Chiefs of Staff, 12 February 1999.

"US, Not UN to lead in post-war Iraq: Rice," 11 February 2004; Available on http://www.abc.net.au/news/newsitems/s825448.htm Internet. Accessed 10 February 2004.

United Nations , *Important Recommendations to Improve Peacekeeping, Planning, Rapid Deployment Already in Place, Under-Secretary – General tells Fourth Committee*, Fifty-sixth General Assembly, Fourth Committee, 20th Meeting. New York, 2001).

United Nations, Security Council. *Resolution 1483 (2003)*, Statement by Benson V. Sevan, Executive Director of the Iraq Programme, 4851st Meeting. New York, 28 October 2003.

United Nations, Security Council. *Resolution 1500 (2003),* Adopted by the Security Council at its 4808th meeting. New York, 14 August 2003.

United Nations, Security Council. *Resolution 1511 (2003),* Adopted by the Security Council at its 4844th meeting. New York, 16 October 2003.

Wallensteen, Peter. "The Resolution and Transformation of International Conflicts: a Structural Perspective." In *New Directions In Conflict Theory, Conflict Resolution and Conflict Transformation*, ed. Raimo Vayrynen, 129-152. London: International Social Science Council, 1991.

Watkins, Eric. "US Officials Underscore Need to Improve Security In Postwar Iraq." *Oil & Gas Journal*, VOL 101, Iss 22, (Jun 2003), p 32.

White, Thomas, Robert C. Kelly, John M. Cape, and Denise Youngblood Coleman. "Reconstructing Eden: A Comprehensive Plan for the Post-War Political and Economic Development in Iraq." 100-250. Houston: Country Watch, 2003.

Whitelaw, Kevin. "Humpty Dumpty Time: Iraqis Face Daunting Obstacles to Remaking Their Economy." *U.S. News and World Report*, 8 December 2003, pp 24-25.

Wolfowitz, Paul. Authority of the Administrator of the Coalition Provisional Authority and Support Relationships." Washington DC: Department of Defense, 16 January 2003.

Wright, Robin and Alissa J. Rubin. "U.S.-Iraq synergy Growing, Official Says." *Los Angeles Times*, 25 September 2003.

Wright, Robin and Anthony Shadid. "U.S. Seeks A Faster Transition In Iraq." *Washington Post*, 12 November 2003, p 1.

Wright, Robin and Colum Lynch. "U.S. Plans New Iraq Proposal for U.N." *Washington Post*, 19 November 2003, p 1.

Wright, Robin and Daniel Williams, "U.S. Moves to Salvage Transition: Bremer to Confer with Top Officials." Washington Post, 16 January 2004, p 1.

Wyatt, Edward. "Clark Proposes Transferring Military Operations IN Iraq To A NATO Force." *New York Times*, 7 November 2003, p 1.

www.ingramcontent.com/pod-product-compliance
Lightning Source LLC
Chambersburg PA
CBHW081804280526
45789CB00008B/2996